OCT
OCT

DI

YOUNG PROFILES

Lindsay Lohan

Jill C. Wheeler
ABDO Publishing Company

visit us at
www.abdopub.com

Published by ABDO Publishing Company, 4940 Viking Drive, Edina, Minnesota 55435. Copyright © 2005 by Abdo Consulting Group, Inc. International copyrights reserved in all countries. No part of this book may be reproduced in any form without written permission from the publisher. The Checkerboard Library™ is a trademark and logo of ABDO Publishing Company.

Printed in the United States.

Cover Photo: Corbis
Interior Photos: Corbis pp. 4, 5, 9, 10, 11, 14, 20, 22, 23, 28-29; Getty Images pp. 7, 13, 15, 16, 17, 19, 21, 25, 27

Editors: Heidi M. Dahmes, Stephanie Hedlund, Megan Murphy
Art Direction: Neil Klinepier

Library of Congress Cataloging-in-Publication Data

Wheeler, Jill C., 1964-
　　Lindsay Lohan / Jill C. Wheeler
　　　　p. cm. -- (Young profiles)
　　Includes index.
　　ISBN 1-59197-878-5
　　1. Lohan, Lindsay, 1986- 2. Actors--United States--Biography--Juvenile literature. I. Title. II. Series.

PN2287.L623W48 2005
791.4302'8'092--dc22
[B]
　　　　　　　　　　　　　　　　　　　　　　　　　　　　2004052928

Contents

Teen Queen 4
Profile of Lindsay Lohan 6
Miniature Model 8
The Parent Trap 10
Another Classic 14
Singing Star 16
Confessions 18
Mean Girls 20
In the Studio 22
Teen Life 24
Coming Up Next 26
Glossary 30
Web Sites 31
Index 32

Teen Queen

Lindsay Lohan is one busy celebrity. In spring 2004, she had two films in theaters. She was **negotiating** to make four more. She was also in the music studio recording her first album.

Lindsay was busy outside the movie and music studios, too. She hosted *Saturday Night Live* and the *2004 MTV Movie Awards*. She also appeared on many talk shows. They included *The Tonight Show with Jay Leno* and *The Sharon Osbourne Show*.

Lindsay wins the Breakthrough Female Award at the 2004 MTV Movie Awards.

Such a schedule might be too much for many people. Yet Lindsay is used to it. She has been in show business since age three. And, fans are likely to see a lot more of her in the coming years. Lindsay's career is taking off with no signs of stopping.

Lindsay signs autographs for her fans.

Profile of Lindsay Lohan

Name: Lindsay Morgan Lohan
Date of Birth: July 2, 1986
Place of Birth: New York City, New York
Current Home: Los Angeles, California
Height: Five feet, six inches
Hair: Red
Eyes: Green
Parents: Michael and Dina Lohan
Siblings: Brothers Michael Jr. and Dakota, and sister Aliana
Favorite Actresses: Jodie Foster and Julia Roberts
Favorite Musicians: Jennifer Lopez and Christina Aguilera
Quote from Lindsay: "Don't change who you are to be accepted."

Miniature Model

Lindsay Morgan Lohan was born on July 2, 1986, in New York City. Her father, Michael, was a Wall Street **trader**. He also helped run his family's pasta business. Lindsay's mother, Dina, was a former **Radio City Music Hall** Rockette.

Michael had been a child actor. Dina was familiar with show business from her experience as a Rockette. So, it seemed natural when Lindsay entered the entertainment world as well.

Lindsay was just three years old when she began modeling. She was signed by the **prestigious** Ford Modeling Agency. In fact, she was the agency's first redheaded model.

The miniature star appeared in advertisements for Abercrombie & Fitch and Calvin Klein. Lindsay also acted in more than 60 television commercials. These advertisements

included **spots** for Pizza Hut, Wendy's, and the Gap.

Lindsay made the leap from commercials to television roles in 1996. She joined the cast of the daytime drama *Another World*. Lindsay was the third young actress to play the role of Alexandra Fowler on the show.

Lindsay began appearing in television commercials at a young age. She even starred in a Jell-O commercial with actor Bill Cosby.

The Parent Trap

By age 11, Lindsay had tackled modeling, commercials, and television. Movies were the next step. In 1998, Disney decided to remake its 1961 classic *The Parent Trap*. The film is about twins who have been separated by their parents' divorce.

The original Parent Trap *starred Hayley Mills.*

The **producers auditioned** about 4,000 hopeful young starlets to play the twins. They invited just five actresses to Los Angeles for a **screen test**. Lindsay was one of the five.

Movie director Nancy Meyers liked what she saw in Lindsay. She said the young actress had a natural talent for comedies. She cast Lindsay to play the dual role of Hallie Parker and Annie

James. Disney also signed Lindsay to a three-movie contract at this time.

Lindsay received several awards for *The Parent Trap*. She earned a Young Artist Award for Leading Actress in a Feature Film. She was also nominated for a YoungStar Award and a Blockbuster Entertainment Award.

For the 1998 remake of The Parent Trap, *the producers wanted to find someone as talented as Mills had been.*

Next, Disney **producers** offered Lindsay the role of Penny in the 1999 *Inspector Gadget* movie. But she turned it down. She had spent more than seven months making *The Parent Trap*. She wanted to be a normal kid. Her parents also wanted her back in school.

However, Lindsay did star with model Tyra Banks in *Life-Size*. The film was a made-for-television Disney production. It was released on video in 2000.

In her next role, Lindsay was back on television. She was cast in Bette Midler's comedy show, *Bette*. But before filming began, the show's producers moved the set from New York City to Los Angeles. Lindsay did not want to leave home quite yet. So, she only appeared in the **pilot** episode.

In 2001, Lindsay still had one more Disney movie in her contract. So she filmed *Get a Clue*. Then she took a break from acting.

Lindsay was considered one of "Disney's darlings" by age 15.

Another Classic

Jamie Lee Curtis was nominated for a Golden Globe Award for her work playing a crabby teenager in Freaky Friday.

Lindsay's biggest role came about a year after she finished *Get a Clue*. She had been watching other young actresses getting parts, and she realized she missed the work. She also missed the fame.

Then, Disney executives announced they were remaking another classic movie, *Freaky Friday*. It is the story of a mother and daughter who spend a day in each other's bodies. Lindsay landed the role of Anna Coleman. Jamie Lee Curtis played her mother.

Lindsay's family also got involved in *Freaky Friday*. Her mother Dina, sister Aliana, and brother Dakota appeared as **extras**. The three had also been extras in *The Parent Trap*.

Lindsay pictured with her father, Michael (left), and brother, Dakota (below). Michael Lohan also works in the movie industry.

Singing Star

Freaky Friday was one of the hit movies of 2003. The film opened in August and shot to the top of the movie charts. Box office receipts totaled more than $100 million.

The movie also gave Lindsay a special opportunity. She had always dreamed of becoming a singer. In *Freaky Friday*, Anna Coleman plays in a band. In real life, Lindsay performed the song that plays during the final **credits**. It is called "Ultimate."

The *Freaky Friday* sound track found its way to *Billboard* magazine's Top 20 in less than three weeks. Lindsay's first song had become part of a hit CD.

Lindsay on MTV during TRL Breakout Stars Week

Estefan Enterprises liked Lindsay's musical style. The record company signed her to a five-album recording deal right before she signed on to do Freaky Friday.

Confessions

Lindsay's next project was another movie for Disney. It was called *Confessions of a Teenage Drama Queen*. The movie was about an overly dramatic girl named Lola. Lola's family moves from the city to the **suburbs**. She must learn that everything does not revolve around her.

Disney originally wanted Hilary Duff to play the lead role of Lola. Instead, Duff accepted the lead in *A Cinderella Story*. That left the part open for Lindsay.

Confessions came out in theaters in early 2004. **Critics** were not very fond of the movie. Yet, they admired Lindsay's acting ability. And by that time, Lindsay was already hard at work on her next project.

Opposite page: Confessions of a Teenage Drama Queen *is based on the novel by Dyan Sheldon. Fans can read more about Lola in Sheldon's new book* My Perfect Life.

Mean Girls

Lindsay at the historic Cinerama Dome on Hollywood's Sunset Boulevard for the premiere of Mean Girls

Lindsay had started filming a movie called *Mean Girls*. The film is about how girls can be really cruel to each other. Lindsay's director from *Freaky Friday*, Mark Waters, directed *Mean Girls*, too. Lindsay also sang some songs on the sound track.

Lindsay plays Cady Heron in the movie. Cady had always been homeschooled. Her life gets a lot harder when she begins classes at an Illinois high school. Her character gets picked on, but then becomes mean herself to get revenge.

Bullying and gossiping are common problems for many teens. Lindsay says she feels lucky those things did not happen to her in real life. She says it helped that she stayed busy in sports, cheerleading, and art.

Saturday Night Live star Tina Fey wrote the Mean Girls screenplay. Fey also plays the role of a teacher in the movie.

In the Studio

Right now, college is on hold for Lindsay. But a singing career is not. Lindsay says she wants to focus more on her career and possibly go to college later.

In spring 2004, Lindsay began recording an album. *American Idol* judge Randy Jackson provided some lyrics. Lindsay wrote some of her own and also worked on playing the guitar. She describes her style as a blend of hip-hop and rock.

Lindsay says singing has long been her first love. She hopes that her fans do not see her as just an actress trying to sing. So, she wants to take the time to do her first album right. It could be at least six months before it is done.

Randy Jackson

Lindsay enjoys the fame her career has brought her.

Teen Life

Lindsay recently moved to Los Angeles, California. She lives in an apartment with fellow actress Raven. Lindsay is still close to her family. In fact, her mother helps manage her career.

Even though she is a celebrity, Lindsay acts a lot like other teens. She enjoys hanging out with her friends, shopping at the mall, and going to movies. Lindsay loves junk food, such as chips and soda.

Many people think Lindsay looks older than she is. Yet she believes it is important to remember her age. She says she does not drink alcohol or party all night. Lindsay also wants to wait until she is older to sing more mature songs and wear certain clothes.

Opposite page: Lindsay has starred in six Disney productions. She says she tries to portray an image that is in line with Disney's family values.

Coming Up Next

What is next for Lindsay? More movies! Lindsay is starring in the film *Dramarama*. It is about a gifted drama student who moves from private school to public school. The movie is expected to be released in late 2004.

Lindsay is also **negotiating** to take a role in another high school film. It is called *Love and Death at Terrington Prep*. Following that project, Lindsay is expected to begin shooting *Herbie: Fully Loaded*. The movie is about a lovable Volkswagen Beetle with a mind of its own.

For Lindsay, it seems unlikely the movie offers will stop anytime soon. Her music career could launch at any time. Lindsay has a long and bright future ahead.

Opposite page: *Lindsay says she admires actresses such as Julia Roberts and Jodie Foster. She wants to follow what they've done, but in her own way.*

Glossary

audition - a short performance to test someone's ability.

credits - a list of people who help with a performance, usually viewed at the end of a movie.

critic - a professional who gives his or her opinion on art or performances.

extra - a person hired to act in a group scene in a movie.

negotiate - to work out an agreement about the terms of a contract.

pilot - a television episode created as a sample of a proposed series.

prestigious - highly regarded, known for excellence.

producer - a person who supervises or provides money for a play, television show, movie, or album.

Radio City Music Hall - a New York City music and dance theater. The production typically features showgirls called Rockettes.

screen test - filming a small part of a movie to see if a person is right for a role.

spot - a short announcement or advertisement in radio, television programs, or magazines.

suburb - the towns or villages just outside a city.

trader - a person who buys and sells on the stock market.

Web Sites

To learn more about Lindsay Lohan, visit ABDO Publishing Company on the World Wide Web at **www.abdopub.com**. Web sites about Lindsay are featured on our Book Links page. These links are routinely monitored and updated to provide the most current information available.

Index

A
American Idol 22
awards 11

B
Banks, Tyra 12

C
Cinderella Story, A 18
commercials 8, 9, 10
Confessions of a Teenage Drama Queen 18
Curtis, Jamie Lee 14

D
Disney 10, 11, 12, 14, 18
Dramarama 26
Duff, Hilary 18

F
family 8, 12, 15, 24
Ford Modeling Agency 8
Freaky Friday 14, 15, 16, 20

G
Get a Clue 12, 14

H
Herbie: Fully Loaded 26

I
Inspector Gadget 12

J
Jackson, Randy 22

L
Life-Size 12
Los Angeles, California 10, 12, 24
Love and Death at Terrington Prep 26

M
Mean Girls 20
Meyers, Nancy 10
Midler, Bette 12
modeling 8, 10
music 4, 16, 20, 22, 24, 26

N
New York City, New York 8, 12

P
Parent Trap, The 10, 11, 12, 15

R
Raven 24

S
Saturday Night Live 4
Sharon Osbourne Show, The 4

T
television roles 9, 10, 12
Tonight Show with Jay Leno, The 4
2004 MTV Movie Awards 4

W
Waters, Mark 20